LEARN THE VALUE OF

Kindness

by Elaine P. Goley

Illustrated by Debbie Crocker

Carmel, New York 10512

© 1987 Rourke Enterprises, Inc.

All rights reserved. No part of this book may be reproduced or utilized in any form or by any means, electronic or mechanical including photocopying, recording or by any information storage and retrieval system without permission in writing from the publisher.

This special Guideposts edition is published by arrangement with Rourke Enterprises, Inc., Vero Beach, FL 32964

Additional material copyright © 1989 by Guideposts Associates, Inc., Carmel, New York 10512

Kindness

Do you know what **kindness** is?

Kindness is giving your little sister one of your favorite toys to play with.

Kindness is giving your cat fresh food and water every day.

Finding Grandpa's reading glasses for him is **kindness**.

Kindness is introducing your new neighbor to your friends.

Helping the teacher erase the blackboards after class is **kindness.**

Kindness is sharing your crayons, even your favorite blue one, with your friend.

Helping your mom with the dishes when she is tired is **kindness.**

Kindness is reading a bedtime story to your little sister.

Hugging your dad and telling him you missed him when he comes home from work is **kindness.**

Playing checkers with your friend when he's sick is **kindness.**

Kindness is setting the table for your mom even before she asks you.

Kindness is thanking Grandma for a birthday present she made just for you.

Kindness is telling someone you'll always be best friends.

Taking your dog for a walk every day is **kindness**.

Kindness is teaching your little brother to tie his shoes.

Kindness is telling your mom she's the best mom in the whole world.

Kindness is thinking about others.

Be ye kind one to another.
>—Ephesians 4:32

David and Jonathan were longtime friends. Now that he had become a powerful king, David wanted to do a good deed for someone in his friend's family. So he questioned a servant of Jonathan's household.

"Is there someone in the family to whom I may show God's kindness?" he asked.

"Well," said the servant, "there is Jonathan's son, Mephibosheth. He has trouble walking because he is crippled."

"Send him to me," the king ordered.

When Mephibosheth appeared before him, King David announced, "For the sake of your father I am returning to you all the land that once belonged to your grandfather. And you are invited to live here at the palace, where life will be easier and you will have servants to wait on you."

So Mephibosheth moved into the king's home and enjoyed a better life.

How did David show **kindness** to Mephibosheth?
Why should you show **kindness**?

This story is from the Bible, the Book of 2 Samuel, chapter 9.

A NOTE TO THE READER

This book was selected by the same editors who prepare *Guideposts*, a monthly magazine filled with true stories of people's adventures in faith.

If you have found inspiration in this book, we think you'll find monthly help and inspiration in the exciting stories that appear in our magazine.

Guideposts is not sold on the newsstand. It's available by subscription only. And subscribing is easy. All you have to do is write Guideposts Associates, Inc., 39 Seminary Hill Road, Carmel, New York 10512. A year's subscription costs only $8.95 in the United States, $10.95 in Canada and overseas.

When you subscribe, each month you can count on receiving exciting new evidence of God's presence and His abiding love for His people.